ORLANDO MAGIC

CONNOR STRATTON

Apex is distributed by North Star Editions:
sales@northstareditions.com | 888-417-0195

Produced for Apex by Red Line Editorial.

Photographs ©: Phelan M. Ebenhack/AP Images, cover, 1, 4–5, 29, 57, 58–59; Rich Storry/Getty Images Sport/Getty Images, 6–7; Focus On Sport/Getty Images Sport/Getty Images, 8–9, 20–21; Al Messerschmidt/AP Images, 10–11; Allsport USA/Getty Images Sport/Getty Images, 12–13, 22–23; Doug Pensinger/Getty Images Sport/Getty Images, 14–15; Ronald Martinez/Getty Images Sport/Getty Images, 16–17; Chris O'Meara/AP Images, 19; Andy Lyons/Allsport/Getty Images Sport/Getty Images, 24–25; Doug Benc/Getty Images Sport/Getty Images, 26–27; Jeff Zelevansky/Getty Images Sport/Getty Images, 30–31; Mitchell Leff/Getty Images Sport/Getty Images, 32–33; Katelyn Mulcahy/Getty Images Sport/Getty Images, 34–35; Jason Miller/Getty Images Sport/Getty Images, 36–37; Sam Greenwood/Getty Images Sport/Getty Images, 38–39; Douglas P. DeFelice/Getty Images Sport/Getty Images, 40–41; Aaron Gash/AP Images, 42–43; Maddie Meyer/Getty Images Sport/Getty Images, 44–45; Mike Ehrmann/Getty Images Sport/Getty Images, 47; Julio Aguilar/Getty Images Sport/Getty Images, 48–49; Cassy Athena/Getty Images Sport/Getty Images, 50–51; Peter Cosgrove/AP Images, 52–53; Ezra Shaw/Getty Images Sport/Getty Images, 54–55

Library of Congress Control Number: 2025944059

ISBN
979-8-89250-914-5 (hardcover)
979-8-89250-945-9 (paperback)
979-8-89824-021-9 (ebook pdf)
979-8-89250-976-3 (hosted ebook)

Printed in the United States of America
Mankato, MN
012026

NOTE TO PARENTS AND EDUCATORS

Apex books are designed to build literacy skills in striving readers. Exciting, high-interest content attracts and holds readers' attention. The text is carefully leveled to allow students to achieve success quickly.

TABLE OF CONTENTS

Paolo Banchero had 13 rebounds against the Pacers on October 28, 2024.

CHAPTER 1

RACKING UP POINTS

The Orlando Magic trailed the Indiana Pacers by five points. Six minutes remained in the game. Orlando forward Paolo Banchero faked toward the basket. Then he stepped back for a jumper. The shot hit nothing but net.

Banchero's shot helped the Magic win 119–115. And he finished the game with 50 points. It was the first time in 20 years that a Magic player had scored 50 points. Fans couldn't wait for more explosive games from their young superstar.

TIKTOK MAGIC

In 1989, the Orlando Magic got a theme song for player introductions. Over time, the team stopped using the song. But in 2023, they started again. The Magic began posting a meme on TikTok after every win. The song plays over the meme.

Jalen Suggs scored 25 points in Orlando's victory over the Pacers.

CHAPTER 2

EARLY HISTORY

In the late 1980s, the National Basketball Association (NBA) added four new teams. The Orlando Magic were one of them. They joined the league in 1989. At first, the Magic struggled. They had losing records in their first three seasons.

Scott Skiles won the Most Improved Player Award in the 1990–91 season.

Orlando's luck changed in 1992. That year, the team had the first pick in the NBA Draft. The Magic selected center Shaquille O'Neal. In 1994, O'Neal helped the Magic make the playoffs for the first time. The next year, they reached their first NBA Finals. However, the Magic fell to the Houston Rockets.

WHAT A NIGHT

The Magic played a memorable game on April 23, 1993. Nick Anderson scored 50 points off the bench. That set an NBA record for a bench player. In the same game, O'Neal took down the whole hoop with a monster dunk.

Shaquille O'Neal averaged 23.4 points and 13.9 rebounds per game in his first season.

In the 1995–96 season, Orlando went 60–22. The Magic also made another deep playoff run. But they lost in the conference finals. After that, O'Neal left Orlando. The team kept making the playoffs regularly. But they couldn't get past the first round.

BEHIND THE NAME

Orlando, Florida, is home to Walt Disney World. One part of the park is called the Magic Kingdom. That's where the Magic's name comes from. Millions of people visit Walt Disney World every year.

The 1995–96 Magic set a team record with 60 wins.

In 2003–04, the Magic had a tough season. They posted the worst record in the NBA. However, their struggles had a bright side. The Magic got the first pick in the 2004 draft. They chose Dwight Howard. The star big man helped the Magic become winners again.

HEART AND HUSTLE

Few people expected much from Orlando in the 1999–2000 season. But the Magic surprised the league. They played hard every game. They ended up going 41–41. People called the team "Heart and Hustle."

Dwight Howard averaged 18.4 points per game with the Magic.

Hedo Türkoğlu averaged 18 points per game in the 2009 Finals.

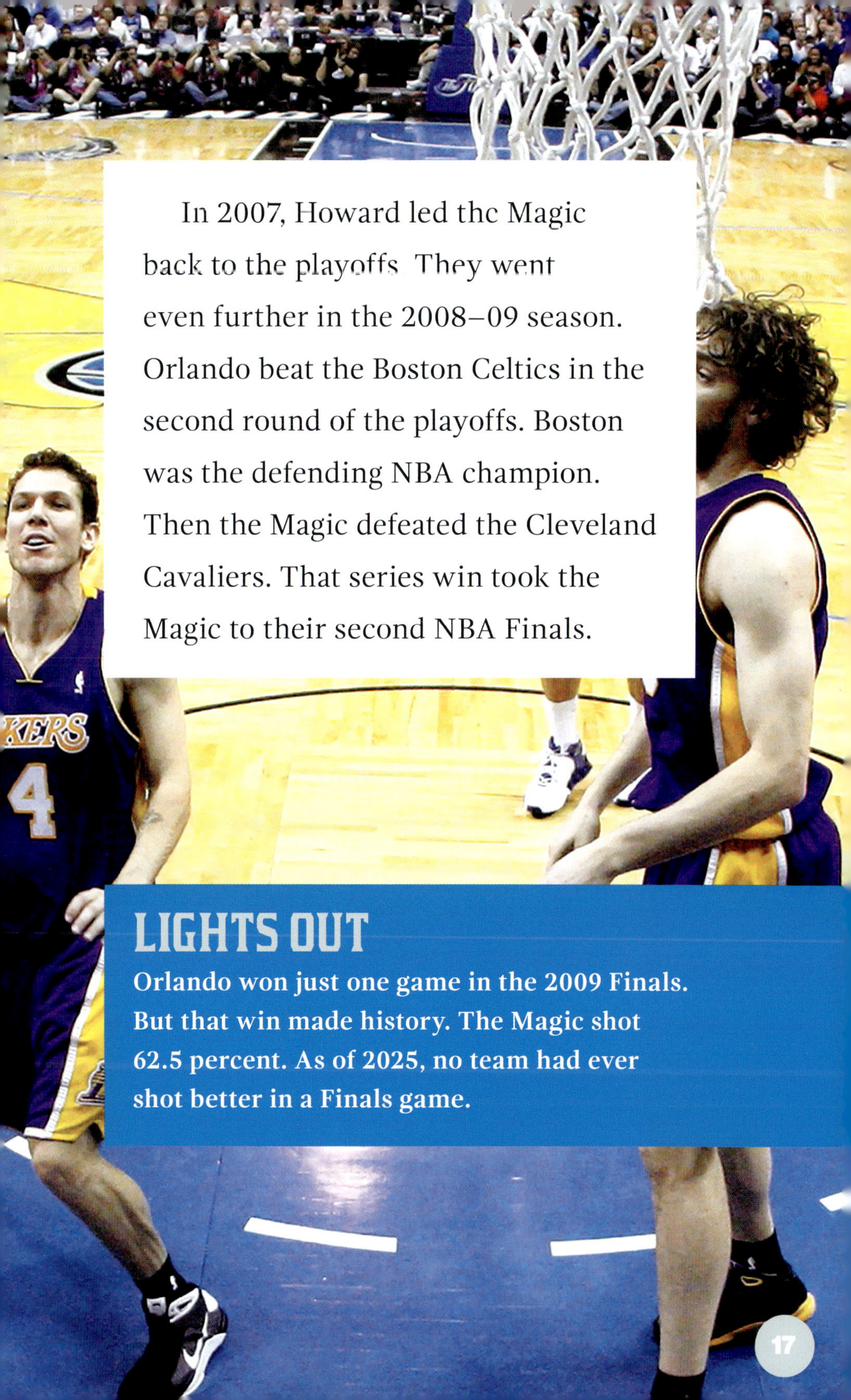

In 2007, Howard led the Magic back to the playoffs. They went even further in the 2008–09 season. Orlando beat the Boston Celtics in the second round of the playoffs. Boston was the defending NBA champion. Then the Magic defeated the Cleveland Cavaliers. That series win took the Magic to their second NBA Finals.

LIGHTS OUT

Orlando won just one game in the 2009 Finals. But that win made history. The Magic shot 62.5 percent. As of 2025, no team had ever shot better in a Finals game.

PLAYER SPOTLIGHT

SHAQUILLE O'NEAL

Shaquille O'Neal was one of the greatest NBA players ever. The All-Star center stood seven feet, one inch (216 cm) tall. He weighed 325 pounds (147 kg). And he was fast for such a huge player.

Right away, O'Neal improved the Magic. He earned the Rookie of the Year Award in the 1992–93 season. And he led the NBA in scoring in 1994–95. That season, O'Neal lifted the Magic to their first NBA Finals.

IN 2016, SHAQUILLE O'NEAL ENTERED THE BASKETBALL HALL OF FAME.

32

CHAPTER 3

LEGENDS

Nick Anderson played a major role on Orlando's early teams. By 1992, he was a top scorer for the Magic. In his 10 seasons with the team, Anderson scored more than 10,000 points.

Nick Anderson shot 45.4 percent over 10 seasons with the Magic.

The Magic picked up Anfernee "Penny" Hardaway in 1993. The rookie quickly became a top point guard. Hardaway often scored over smaller players. And he was an excellent playmaker.

THIRTY DIMES

Scott Skiles was a key part of the early Magic years. He was known for his passing skills. In 1990, Skiles dished out 30 assists in one game. As of 2025, that was still an NBA record.

Anfernee Hardaway made the All-NBA First Team twice with Orlando.

Tracy McGrady won the Most Improved Player Award in the 2000–01 season.

Tracy McGrady carried the Magic in the early 2000s. McGrady was dangerous from anywhere on the court. He led the NBA in scoring twice. In a 2004 game, he recorded 62 points. No Magic player had ever scored more in a game.

THREES ALL DAY

Defenders swarmed O'Neal and Hardaway in the 1990s. That left other players on the team wide open. In 1996, Dennis Scott dropped 11 three-pointers in one game. That set an NBA record.

Jameer Nelson averaged 5.4 assists per game with the Magic.

After O'Neal left, Dwight Howard filled his shoes. Howard had plenty of help, too. Hedo Türkoğlu was one of the NBA's first point forwards. That is a forward who runs the offense like a point guard. Jameer Nelson also racked up assist after assist. Meanwhile, Rashard Lewis scored from long range.

GAME-WINNERS

Hedo Türkoğlu's clutch scoring helped the Magic during the 2009 playoffs. He hit a game-winning three to beat the Philadelphia 76ers. Then he scored another game-winner in Game 4 against the Celtics.

PLAYER SPOTLIGHT

DWIGHT HOWARD

Few players could match Dwight Howard's athletic ability. The center scored easily in the paint. He became Orlando's all-time points leader. However, Howard was best known for his defense. He led the league in blocks two seasons in a row.

Howard was also the NBA's leading rebounder five times. He averaged 13.0 rebounds per game with the Magic. Howard's two-way presence carried the Magic to their second NBA Finals in 2009.

DWIGHT HOWARD EARNED DEFENSIVE PLAYER OF THE YEAR HONORS IN THREE STRAIGHT SEASONS.

12
DALLAS
2

CHAPTER 4

RECENT HISTORY

Dwight Howard kept the Magic in the playoffs after their 2009 run. But they couldn't get back to the Finals. Then, in 2012, Orlando traded Howard.

As a member of the Magic, Dwight Howard averaged 19.9 points per game in the playoffs.

The Magic received Nikola Vučević as part of the Howard trade. The center was a star for the rest of the 2010s. Even so, the Magic struggled. From the 2012–13 season to the 2017–2018 season, Orlando was one of the worst teams in the NBA.

NEW REBOUND KING

In 1993, Shaquille O'Neal grabbed 28 rebounds in one game. That team record stood for nearly 20 years. Nikola Vučević broke it in 2012. He pulled down 29 rebounds. Vučević scored 20 points in that game, too.

Nikola Vučević averaged 10.8 rebounds per game with the Magic.

Jalen Suggs became one of Orlando's best defenders in the 2020s.

Steve Clifford became Orlando's head coach in 2018. He led the Magic to their first winning record since 2012. The team reached the playoffs two years in a row. But both times, the Magic fell in the first round. Then injuries slowed the team in the 2020–21 season.

BIG TRADE

In 2021, the Magic traded Nikola Vučević to the Chicago Bulls. They got two draft picks in return. Orlando used one pick on Franz Wagner. The Magic also picked up Jalen Suggs that year. Both players helped Orlando become contenders again.

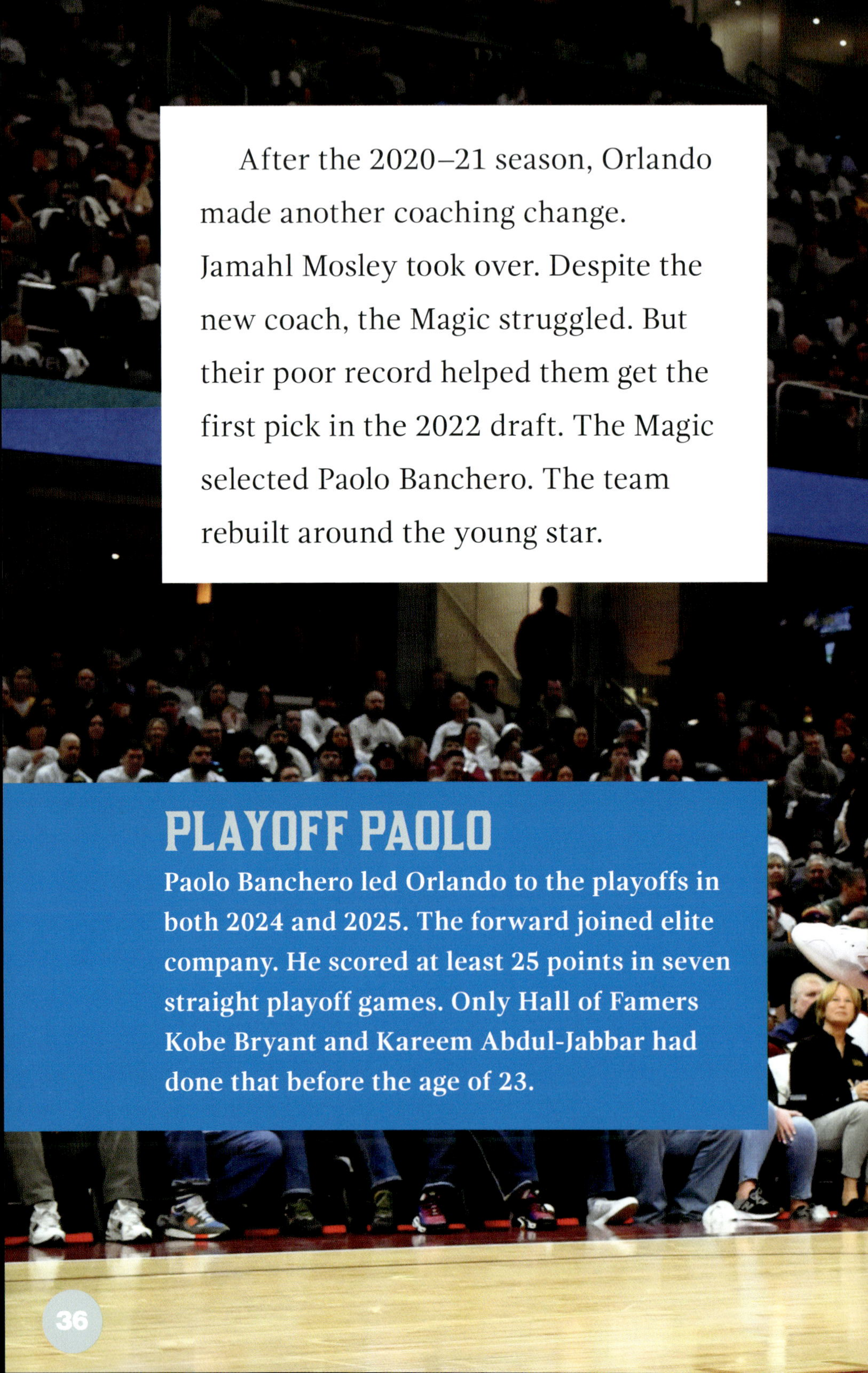

After the 2020–21 season, Orlando made another coaching change. Jamahl Mosley took over. Despite the new coach, the Magic struggled. But their poor record helped them get the first pick in the 2022 draft. The Magic selected Paolo Banchero. The team rebuilt around the young star.

PLAYOFF PAOLO

Paolo Banchero led Orlando to the playoffs in both 2024 and 2025. The forward joined elite company. He scored at least 25 points in seven straight playoff games. Only Hall of Famers Kobe Bryant and Kareem Abdul-Jabbar had done that before the age of 23.

Paolo Banchero attempts a layup during a 2024 playoff game against the Cleveland Cavaliers.

CHAPTER 5

MODERN STARS

In the late 2000s, Orlando had many great players. JJ Redick spent seven seasons with the Magic. He shot nearly 40 percent from three-point range. Vince Carter and Ryan Anderson were two other stars. Their scoring provided a boost during Dwight Howard's final years with the team.

Ryan Anderson won the Most Improved Player Award for the 2011–12 season.

Nikola Vučević became Orlando's next star center. Vučević played in Orlando for nearly a decade. He was a bright spot during a tough stretch for the Magic. He averaged a double-double with Orlando.

SCORING FROM ALL OVER

Evan Fournier and Aaron Gordon joined the Magic in 2014. Fournier scored efficiently from outside. Gordon brought toughness in the paint. He was an amazing dunker.

In the 2019–20 season, Evan Fournier averaged a career-high 18.5 points per game.

In the 2021–22 season, rookies Franz Wagner and Jalen Suggs energized Orlando. Wagner's footwork helped him cut through defenses as he drove to the basket. Meanwhile, Suggs took the Magic's defense to another level.

THE WAGNER BROTHERS

Moritz "Moe" Wagner played for the University of Michigan in college. So did his brother Franz Wagner. Both brothers made it to the NBA. In 2021, they both joined the Magic.

Moe (21) and Franz (22) Wagner played together for the first time as professionals with the Magic.

In the 2024–25 season, Jalen Suggs averaged 1.5 steals per game.

In the early 2020s, the Magic became known for their defense. Their centers guarded the rim and grabbed rebounds. Guards Jalen Suggs and Anthony Black defended farther out.

Veteran Kentavious Caldwell-Pope joined the Magic for the 2024–25 season. He locked down opponents. That season, the Magic allowed fewer than 106 points per game. That was the lowest average in the league.

PLAYER SPOTLIGHT

PAOLO BANCHERO

Paolo Banchero had the size and strength of a forward. But he played with a guard's touch. He immediately became the Magic's top scorer.

Scoring wasn't Banchero's only talent. He crashed the boards to grab rebounds. He found open teammates when he was double-teamed. And he improved his defense each season.

Banchero shined in his first two years in the playoffs. He averaged 28 points per game. And he shot 42 percent from three-point range.

PAOLO BANCHERO WON THE ROOKIE OF THE YEAR AWARD IN THE 2022–23 SEASON.

ORLANDO
5

CHAPTER 6

TEAM TRIVIA

The Magic's arena is in downtown Orlando. It opened in 2010. At the time, the arena had the biggest video screen in the NBA. It was also the first energy-efficient arena in the league. The building tries to save energy and water.

The Magic's arena holds more than 18,500 fans.

Orlando has had the same mascot since the team's first season.

Orlando's mascot is a green dragon. His name is Stuff the Magic Dragon. The name is based on the song "Puff, the Magic Dragon." The name relates to basketball, too. *Stuff* is another word for a slam dunk.

DANGEROUS DUNKS

The Magic have a great history of dunking. Shaquille O'Neal broke two hoops in his career. In response, the NBA built stronger hoops. In 2009, Dwight Howard dunked so hard that the shot clock on the backboard broke.

Shaquille O'Neal made the All-Star team every season that he played with the Magic.

The Magic's colors are blue, black, and white. Many of their jerseys feature thin stripes. And they often use a star for the letter *A*. In 2025, the Magic came out with new jerseys. The design was an update on some of the team's first jerseys from the 1990s.

O'NEAL'S ONLY THREE

Shaquille O'Neal played for several teams over his 19-year career. He scored more than 11,000 field goals during that time. However, only one of them was a three-pointer. Shaq hit a long-range buzzer-beater for the Magic in 1996.

The Miami Heat joined the NBA one year before the Magic. The two teams were the only NBA teams in Florida. This began the "Sunshine State" rivalry. The Heat remain Orlando's biggest rival.

DUNKING CHAMPS

In 2025, Mac McClung won his third straight Slam Dunk Contest. He's the second player in Magic history to win it. The first was Dwight Howard in 2008. That year, "Superman" wore a cape during one of his dunks.

Mac McClung was the first player to win three Slam Dunk Contests in a row.

TEAM RECORDS

All-Time Points: **11,435**
Dwight Howard (2004–12)

All-Time Assists: **3,501**
Jameer Nelson (2004–14)

All-Time Rebounds: **8,072**
Dwight Howard (2004–12)

All-Time Steals: **1,004**
Nick Anderson (1989–99)

All-Time Blocks: **1,344**
Dwight Howard (2004–12)

All-Time Three-Pointers: **981**
Dennis Scott (1990–97)

All-Time Triple-Doubles: **8**
Elfrid Payton (2014–18)

All-Time Games Played: **692**
Nick Anderson (1989–99)

All-Time Minutes Played: **22,471**
Dwight Howard (2004–12)

All-Time Coaching Wins: **267**
Brian Hill (1993–97, 2005–07)

** All statistics are accurate through the 2024–25 season.*

MAGIC
12
DALLAS
2

TIMELINE

1989 — The Orlando Magic begin playing their first season in the NBA.

1992 — The Magic draft Shaquille O'Neal with the first overall pick.

1995 — The Magic defeat the Chicago Bulls on their way to their first NBA Finals.

2000 — The "Heart and Hustle" Magic surprise the league and nearly make the playoffs.

2004 — Orlando selects Dwight Howard with the first pick in the draft.

2009

Howard leads the Magic to their second Finals, but they lose to the Los Angeles Lakers.

2012

Howard leaves Orlando. The Magic miss the playoffs for the next six seasons.

2021

Jamahl Mosley becomes head coach, and the Magic begin rebuilding with rookies Franz Wagner and Jalen Suggs.

2022

The Magic use the first overall pick to draft Paolo Banchero, who wins Rookie of the Year honors.

2025

Banchero leads the Magic to the playoffs for the second year in a row.

COMPREHENSION QUESTIONS

Write your answers on a separate piece of paper.

1. Write a paragraph that explains the main ideas of Chapter 2.
2. Who do you think was the greatest player in Magic history? Why?
3. Who broke Shaquille O'Neal's single-game rebounding record in 2012?
   A. Paolo Banchero
   B. Dwight Howard
   C. Nikola Vučević
4. What showed the strength of the Magic's defense in the 2024–25 season?
   A. The Magic allowed the fewest points per game in the NBA.
   B. Paolo Banchero shot well from three-point range in the playoffs.
   C. The Magic released new jerseys.

5. What does **hustle** mean in this book?

*They played hard every game. They ended up going 41–41. People called the team "Heart and **Hustle**."*

A. winning titles
B. moving slowly
C. trying hard

6. What does **elite** mean in this book?

*The forward joined **elite** company. He scored at least 25 points in seven straight playoff games. Only Hall of Famers Kobe Bryant and Kareem Abdul-Jabbar had done that before the age of 23.*

A. the most common
B. the best of the best
C. the youngest

Answer key on page 64.

GLOSSARY

assists
Passes that lead directly to baskets.

buzzer-beater
A shot made with no time left on the game clock.

clutch
Having to do with a difficult situation when the outcome of the game is in question.

conference
A group of teams that make up part of a sports league.

double-double
A game in which a player records at least 10 of two different stats.

draft
A system that lets teams select new players coming into the league.

mascot
A figure that is a symbol of a sports team.

paint
The area between the basket and the free-throw line.

rivalry
An ongoing competition that brings out strong emotion from fans and players.

rookie
An athlete in his or her first year as a professional player.

TO LEARN MORE

BOOKS

Giedd, Steph. *Orlando Magic All-Time Greats.* Press Box Books, 2024.

Hewson, Anthony K. *Orlando Magic.* Abdo Publishing, 2023.

Whiting, Jim. *The Story of the Orlando Magic.* Creative Education, 2023.

ONLINE RESOURCES

Visit **www.apexeditions.com** to find links and resources related to this title.

ABOUT THE AUTHOR

Connor Stratton writes and edits nonfiction children's books. He lives in Minnesota.

INDEX

ANSWER KEY:

1. Answers will vary; 2. Answers will vary; 3. C; 4. A; 5. C; 6. B